R.G. Shelton books may be ordered through booksellers or by contacting:

RGS Publishing
P.O. Box 92860
Washington, DC 20090
www.rgsheltononline.com

ISBN: 978-0-9857188-0-0
ISBN: 978-0-9857188-1-7

Cover design by R.G. Shelton

Book design by R.G. Shelton

RGS Publications

Printed in the United States of America

Second Printing: June 7, 2012

I AM
SHE

R.G. Shelton

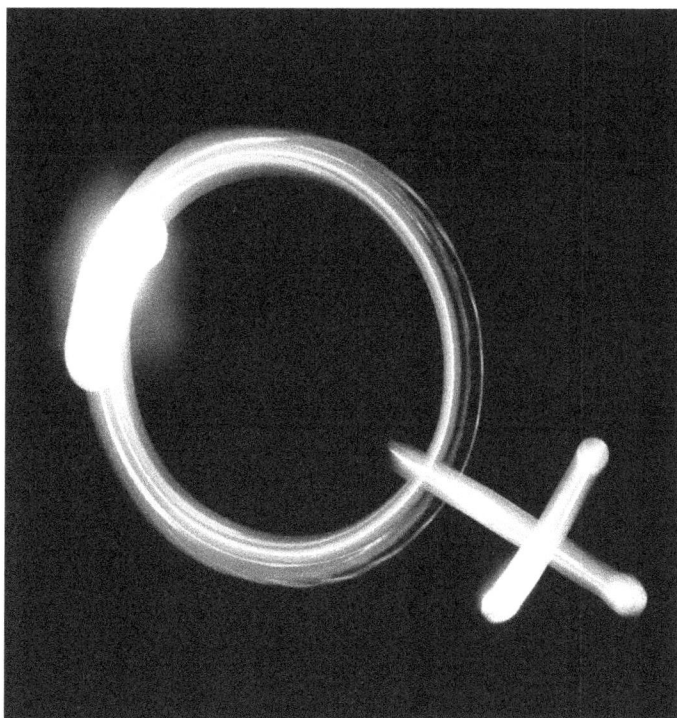

Dedication

I dedicate this to my husband and children who have assisted me in realizing I always have a choice and the power to create and re-create my life. I thank you because you love me just the way I am. I thank you because I experience the greatest love and possibilities of God through you. I love you more than words are able to express.

This is an R.G. Shelton publication
www.rgsheltononline.com

John 14 (NKJV)

The Way, the Truth, and the Life

14 "Let not your heart be troubled; you believe in God, believe also in Me. [2] In My Father's house are many mansions;[a] if *it were* not *so,* I would have told you. I go to prepare a place for you.[b] [3] And if I go and prepare a place for you, I will come again and receive you to Myself; that where I am, *there* you may be also. [4] And where I go you know, and the way you know."

[5] Thomas said to Him, "Lord, we do not know where You are going, and how can we know the way?"

[6] Jesus said to him, "I am the way, the truth, and the life. No one comes to the Father except through Me.

The Father Revealed

[7] "If you had known Me, you would have known My Father also; and from now on you know Him and have seen Him."

[8] Philip said to Him, "Lord, show us the Father, and it is sufficient for us."

[9] Jesus said to him, "Have I been with you so long, and yet you have not known Me, Philip? He who has seen Me has seen the Father; so how can you say, 'Show us the Father'? [10] Do you not believe that I am in the Father, and the Father in Me? The words that I speak to you I do not speak on My own *authority;* but the Father who dwells in Me does the works. [11] Believe Me that I *am* in the Father and the Father in Me, or else believe Me for the sake of the works themselves.

The Answered Prayer

[12] "Most assuredly, I say to you, he who believes in Me, the works that I do he will do also; and greater *works* than these he will do, because I go to My Father. [13] And whatever you ask in My name, that I will do, that the Father may be glorified in the Son. [14] If you ask[c] anything in My name, I will do *it*

John 15 (NKJV)

The True Vine

15 "I am the true vine, and My Father is the vinedresser. [2] Every branch in Me that does not bear fruit He takes away;[a] and every *branch* that bears fruit He prunes, that it may bear more fruit. [3] You are already clean because of the word which I have spoken to you. [4] Abide in Me, and I in you. As the branch cannot bear fruit of itself, unless it abides in the vine, neither can you, unless you abide in Me.

[5] "I am the vine, you *are* the branches. He who abides in Me, and I in him, bears much fruit; for without Me you can do nothing. [6] If anyone does not abide in Me, he is cast out as a branch and is withered; and they gather them and throw *them* into the fire, and they are burned. [7] If you abide in Me, and My words abide in you, you will[b] ask what you desire, and it shall be done for you. [8] By this My Father is glorified, that you bear much fruit; so you will be My disciples.

My Truth Today
(Letter to Myself)

This is my truth. Today I decided to make the right choice for me. Today I decided to be honest with myself even though it says things about me I do not want to believe of myself. I better understand that until I own my truth, no matter how it may look, I cannot disown its reality and the impact it has until I first own it. I am attempting to live as I desire in the fullness of my possibility, but not owning all aspects of me, even those I do not like, stunt and slow down my elevation to the place I envision myself. So I submit to the truth so that it may set me free.

I am a woman, a mother, a wife, a daughter, a friend and sometimes my own enemy. I love to be loved and I love to love. However, I do not desire to be violated, taken advantage of, overworked or frustrated in the process of giving that love or in order to receive love or be anyone else's idea of love in action.

Although this is the standard in which I set for myself, it seems I had blurred the lines somewhere and the feeling of frustration, being overworked, feeling taken advantage of and being others ideas of who I should be appear to be a reality more often than I would like to admit.

1

I know that what I perceived was not anyone's original intent (at least I hope not). However, the reactional sensation felt from within me that was a reflection of my own discontentment was more powerful than their true intent. The consideration for my soul's desire and purpose was forsaken by me more than anyone else I admit today. This was a low standard I set in which others were adhering to and you were only treating me in the manner I allowed.

I have compromised myself in this position and often I just deal with it as "good" wives, mothers and women do. However the feeling this time, this day is so intense I must pay it attention. I must evaluate it. I must look at it closely so that I may understand why I feel this way despite my struggle against it.

The feeling of contradiction cries out deep from within me begging me for the awareness necessary to be free. Today I refuse to push it down again. This is the last day it will rear its head for attention. Today it will be given all of my attention. I want to know about me. What I am doing for me. What I am not doing for me. How it is impacting me at this level of depth that stirs my spirit to cry out so loud.

The times I most desired to be loved, to be loving, to be happy or was the most vulnerable this restlessness in my spirit would hinder me from reaching out for what I most desired and needed from the ones I loved. I would pause for what I needed thinking of what they may not or could not give me. The ideas in my head of what good wives and mother's do impressed upon me to terminate fulfilling my need and internalized a falsehood that I did not matter enough to you because I believed I did not matter enough to be put first in my own life. This "good" deed sowed seeds that are now growing into "bad" vines, more like weeds that entangle and strangle my life, my thoughts and feelings of myself and everyone else.

I put myself on a hiatus of gratification and in turn it stalled me from expressing my greatest desire and receiving my greatest desire – love and validation through love to and from those I love. After all, that would be putting me first and all good wives, mothers and women should think of others first, right?

The feeling of regret, desire to be validated and the hurt that I am not enough and they don't love me the way I desire was standing in my way. It was growing more and more feeding off of the neglect of self. I desired to yell at the top of my lungs that I am more that a woman, a mother, a wife, a daughter and a friend and the expectation and labels these titles came with, they were killing who I truly AM!

I was more than any of these titles could define. These titles limited me to things and duties I do not desire and never desired. These titles and duties actually steal my joy, peace and who I envisioned of myself.

Expectation to live in accordance to other's ideas of who I am was killing me. No matter how much I protested, the expectation never seemed to die and I needed it to. It continued to fall right back on my lap. I realized it was because I cannot kill what another owns. I cannot change their mind. I can only kill what I own. So I have to change. I have to change my mind in order to change my life. I have to change being what others want in order to change their expectation of who I am.

Changing me was the only think that would impact change in anyone else. I came to the point of knowing that all change will only come in reaction to mine. I could no longer fight other's to change. I had to set the standard, take back my power and realize that what is good for me as ME will be the best for everyone.

3

Then and only then would I be a whole person and operating in my wholeness (holiness) will the greatness within me rise to the place of completion of ME. Otherwise I will be my worst enemy and block myself from having what I most desire – Me and the love of Me.

Today I told my family my truth and this is what I said:

"I do not want to wash your clothes. I love a clean and neat home, but I do not desire to clean it every day. I do not desire to wash your dishes, cook your meals, clean your bathrooms, go to the grocery store, figure out what you want to eat and then spend my days and nights making those meals that I don't hunger for. In fact, I am not even hungry.

These pounds I carry are not mine. They are your hungry desires. I am eating what you want to eat and drinking what you want to drink and going where you want to eat and I am carrying your pounds and your stomach aches and today I want you to know I don't want it anymore. I don't care to compromise for anyone outside of me anymore.

Yes, I want to be with you. I want to sit on the couch with you, but not clean around you and cook in the kitchen while everyone else sits on the sofa. I want to ride somewhere and talk. I do not want to drive and wish everyone would shut up so I can think and get my bearings asking me a million mommy questions. I want to have an in-depth conversation and think deep thoughts and not teach and repeat and correct during my entire conversation. I want to know beyond a shadow of a doubt that you will be fine and grow up well if I am not constantly telling you the way, but showing you by being ME.

*So today I no longer am in want. I do not want things to be different, today, I **choose** different. I **choose** not to be every woman* to everyone unless it is my desire coming from me. Not anyone else's desire being reflected upon Me.

I choose not to be all things to you or anyone else including me. I choose to just be. I choose not to be perfect, because your ever changing definition of perfection will have me contorted and distorted all over the place so I choose to be perfectly Me.

Perfectly imperfect in all the perfect places that make me ME. Perfectly perfect in the places that make Me unique. Perfectly disappointing at times and perfectly surprising at times. Perfectly over loving and under serving. Perfectly overzealous at times, but never jealous. Hoping upon my faith and never giving up faith despite what it looks like. Overly optimistic and mind creating ME. Talkative, but still and quiet when it matters most ME. I love ME so much I choose ME today because I love her enough to choose her, in mind, body and soul.

I need Her mind. I desire Her spirit be free and She desires to be ME in body manifestation. We are one perfectly made for each other and if you all were allowed to see Us as one perfectly created wholeness as She, Me, Who I Am, then you would no longer desire or want Me to do for you, give to you, be for you what I am not, but only who I AM. She who cannot be anything else to or for you except Her. You would recognize the holiness in My wholeness.

I am, beautiful, whole, ever changing, ever growing not complete except in Myself. In Herself, full of Herself and not full of anyone or anything other than Herself, Myself. That is who you will desire to be around as well because She is all-ways loving, all-ways forgiving, all-ways passionate, all-ways present, all-ways teaching, all-ways serving, all-ways receiving, all-ways all things because She IS. You will love Her all-ways in all Her ways because all ways of Her are beautiful when She is allowed to be All-ways. Not your way, not their way, not any way, but all Her ways – good, *bad or indifferent does not matter as long as they are My ways, Her ways, Our way.*

I have a path and on that path I am experiencing myself as many things and I love them all, even the ugly and dirty me, because it is helping me to know who I am and who I am not or who I am not any longer. That is what allows me to love you the same way. So I choose my path and I remove myself from your path. I hope this allows you the ability to do your path the way you desire so you can be all of you and know who you are and who you are not because that is the greatest gift you can give me – all of you. All-ways of You.

This person I validate today is who I love, she is love, this is who I am, and this is who I desire. I want to share this true ME with you. I want to be the best mother, wife, sister, daughter and friend in the way that best expresses who I am and not conform to another's idea no matter how much I love them. Because if I do not first *love me,* I cannot love another.

My children, do not judge me or yourself if we don't look like, sound like or conform to the outside world, its norms or ideas. I want to talk to you, not teach you everything. I want to know you, not correct you in all things. I want to walk with you, not lead your path. I want to sit with you, not stand over you and dictate your feelings, emotions, hands or direction.

I want to be and I desire for you to be. I desire the best for you and I desire the best of me for you. I desire to love you and the best of you to love me back. I desire not to wash your clothes, but to wash away the hurt, the fear, the confusion and the past lies by the present love and companionship I bring today.

Dear husband, I don't want to conform your mind, but allow it to be transformed by the renewing of your mind in conversation. I want you to tell me what you know to be true so I can be free to tell you my truth so when we are together and I show you mine and you show me yours it is a reflection of the great intimacy we have had in the mind and spirit level allowing the body to have no bounds of pleasure because we are already naked and have bared our souls and have no judgment, only love, compassion, forgiveness and validation that we are perfect even in our imperfections because we Are One.

I dig deeper and go to another level of honesty within myself and discern that despite all of what I have said, none of what I feel actually has to do with doing or not doing. It definitely does not have to do with you, my family or anyone else outside of myself. It is all about what is going on and not going on within me. This has everything to do with me valuing myself as the child of God I am. I was so busy doing and living for others and forsaking myself, I neglected the fact that I am a child of God with a great purpose and desire that is greater than what I am today. I must serve the God in me and the purpose that God has breathed into me.

I forgot that I was set aside for a purpose. That purpose was not and is not limited to the value system, ideals, definitions or benefit of other limited beings, but for the elevation and unlimited experience of myself and those blessed by the overflow of me being Me. The burden to be what others want to the detriment of who I am I no longer desire to struggle with. I lay this burden at the altar. I give it rest and I give ME life. This is ME, I am SHE and I only need you to hear Her so that you can see Her. Is that okay? Yes, it is because I am the creator of my experience in life and what I name good is good. Today I name me good and more than enough, I name awareness, this choice good. And so it is!

7

Being Free

I wrote the previous letter and this resulting book after feeling overwhelmed in my spirit for about a week or so. This heaviness I felt was not a new feeling. It had come and gone many times in the recent past. However, I was always able to overcome it. I would call myself into a happy and content place, and move right back into the swing of life. This particular time I noticed that this feeling was not going to go away unless I got to the root of it. It felt more like a solid weight, not the usual fleeting sensitivity. It was not going to just pass. There was a spring within me that was not beneficial to me that needed my attention. Its obvious significance grasped my attention and on that day I decided not to forsake its call to me.

After analyzing this feeling for a few days and digging further and further into the soil of my being I realized that with all that I knew I was still forsaking myself in a very important area. I needed to be truthful with myself.

In the past I was able to conquer various levels of my existence, however, there was one place I failed to touch. I had to be still enough to be honest enough about why I would not make a change in this area of my life I now call *compromise*. I thought I was in too deep and could not now change my mind.

Despite that feeling I was curious of my predicament and looked closer at its existence. I conceded there were aspects about me that were contrary to what I believed about myself. I did not want to face that ugly truth about me at that moment. It was a heavy thought to handle. I took another stab at accepting my choices, my compromises and all that came with them.

I wished to be content in my decision to not face the music despite the discomfort my current condition offered me. I told myself the same think I always have since a child – *"Yes, we may have bitten off too much for us to chew, but if we suck it up a few more years it will be okay. Change will come. This is what good girls, good mothers, strong wives, dedicated daughters and loving sisters do. They deal with it, all of it and somehow joy or some other reward will surface from our sacrifice of self."*

That was the lie I needed to be true. The lie I desired to accept. The lie that said doing nothing to change where I was in the hierarchy of my own importance was okay because eventually things would change just because I wanted them to. Can I get any hands that will agree that this strategy that lacks action never works?

This story we have told ourselves and passed down for others to buy is more than ridiculous. I desired a refund on this lie I bought. I preferred to buy another story, another way of being. Better yet, I wished to manufacture a new story that best suited who I am and who I desired to be.

History, role playing, systems and acceptance of these and other limiting authoritative precedence keep many of us in a box. This box appeared to be winning even in my life as I struggled against it.

My ability to buy another idea of myself seemed not possible. My ability to create another idea for myself after participating in the lie prior seemed even more impossible. Somehow I still hoped beyond hope and knew within me it was more than possible. It was a reality I could taste. I believed that if God is outside the box, if He is limitless and can choose to be any and all things then that is where and what I should be able to do. I am that I am. I will be what I will be. That is where my greatness is. In the I am that He is. My greatness is where my God is. But what is that? Where is that? And why am I here outside of the place I desire? These are the questions I knew could bring me the answers that would offer me peace and wholeness to the hole I felt within. The hole informing me that there was a disconnect.

After much contemplation the answers came. After the answers surfaced, I was apprehensive in dealing with the truth they carried. The reality that was staring me in my face I did not want to face. I feared that my truth would not be understood and may be a little unorthodox. Okay, a lot unorthodox. I feared that if I said out loud what I was feeling, seeing and knew within me, that my world would crumble. Though crumbling is what I wanted. I did not want it in the most extreme manner.

As is often the case, I feared the unknown. I feared that my current world would have to disintegrate in order for me to create the world I desired. How that would happen and what it would look like was a scary unknown. I knew what I wanted my world to look like in the end, but what I did not know is what it would look like during the tear down of the current life structure in order to make room for my new life creation. In that small space of unknown transition, my life weighed in the balance and I was left wanting.

I was left wanting because I feared moving past this unknown place. This one place kept me from my promised land. I actually feared getting what I desired. I worried how others impacted by my decision (to put me first in my own life) would react to me no longer being a reactor in their universe, but the creator of my own universe. I feared what it would mean to them. Once again putting them before me. Yes once again worried about everyone else and relinquishing my feelings. Is that not the problem I started out with?

The what, when, where, how and to what extent was all driven by fear. Yes, that good old common enemy, fear. The one thing that stops us, that limits us and keeps us from the greatness we are and experiencing the greatness that is ours.

I had to confront fear. That is the only way fear becomes fearful enough to leave us. This allows us to become fearless enough to create. When we confront fear and realize he is not real, he is a figment of our imagination of possibilities that will usually never be probable. Fear will flee from the fear of exposure. Fear is energized on the power we give it. Fear has not real power. It only has the ability to suggest. When we take our power back with our power of choice he has none. It is as if he is stripped naked before us.

I desired to make a decision based on my truth of what I needed and desired for the wholeness of who I am. The only way to get this was for me to face the fear and be honest with myself and those close to me despite what that truth looked like. My truth had to be said out loud and my life had to be made over in alignment with what my soul desired so that I could be freely ME.

My truth was revelational and soul saving to me. However, when I saw it through the eyes of everyone else, I could see the possibility of how ugly it may appear to them. How unbeneficial to them it could be, despite its great benefit to me. Though it felt good and resonated in my soul, saying it out loud had the ability to sound horrible.

The down and dirty sounded like this – *"I wanted to be a model woman, a wife and mother and I had great expectations for these roles, but currently, I hate every other minute of it. I feel like I was sold a bill of goods not worth the paper it was printed on. I feel like my dreams of being an idyllic woman, a wife and mother have been reduced to everyone else's ideas and your ideas of me suck. They suck really bad and they are killing me more and more every day. I want to live in these roles by the script I write. I am taking my power back. Please move off of my throne. I will rule my own life. I will write the script for the life I desire. Take your pen and do not write another script for me again. Not even a side note. Thanks, I love you. You all are the best."*

After accepting my dilemma and saying it out loud I arrived at a deeper revelation. I recognized why I now disliked the choices I once enjoyed. I disliked them because they led to other choices that manifested the life I was living that did not look like the dream I desired for myself. It looked like the dream that everyone else had for me. Not just my core family, but society's idea of a woman, wife, sister, daughter and mother. These same estimations were taught to me in school, home and church. It was a constant billboard of life telling me who I was and who I was not and no matter how I fought against it, it edged its way right into my life and I was disappointed that I bent one too many times to these ideals only to be saddled by them bent over in extreme insufficiency of myself.

I morphed into the desire of everyone else and I was no longer in my own picture. I was an image of everyone else's creation. I was a shadow in my own dream becoming the nightmare I did not want to face. Facing that shadow of me was too painful. I did not know what to do with her or how to get her back. Since I was not sure how to save her, I let her continue to fade into the background of everyone else's dream, because I was told that is what good mothers, wives, girls and women do.

There was no comfort in the fact that house after house, family after family had replicas of these same faded paintings of dreams deferred on the walls of their lives. Making it appear to be normal despite the abnormality to my soul's consciousness. When I spoke to other women they were sucking it up. They believed that we had

13

to sacrifice life, love and self so that everyone else could have a life, love and be themselves. There was this consensus that we as women make it through these years with that stupid smile on our faces and then one day we would get a life later. What? I could not live with that. That thought was heartbreaking. I was ME right now and had more of ME to give, more things to experience and more to do **RIGHT NOW**, not later.

I did not desire to die right now so everyone else could live. I thought, "*It makes no sense that I give up all now and when I am too tired to care then I would love and live for me?*" That is just stupid. I am a being of the most sophisticated kind. I am a female, the feminine side of God, the place in which life itself dwells and I must give up all I am so that the male and the offspring I birth can have even more than I am or have. I give up the life that I am so that others may live and I have no life left for me. How do I give up all that I am so that others can have and expect to have anything left for me to be me?

I guess that is the problem right there. I give up all so others can live. Yeah, that is the problem, because if I give up all, then I am dead! I am the walking dead! Great! Oh how wonderful to be the willing victim! Did that sound right to you? Being the walking dead makes us a great mother, wife, and woman. Like I said before, that is just unintelligent, daft, dippy, ill-advised thinking. How did we get suckered into this lie? And how many of us are so undervalued that we keep participating in this valueless crucifixion to be valued by other people when the truth is, I was already valued when God breathed life into me. So why am I doing this? Why do I conform to the lie if it kills me to do so? Whose true lie am I living?

I asked God about this lie. I asked about this sacrifice. This mimic of sacrifice we have draped on our shoulders as if it is the greatest we can be. And I got the answer – God said "*everyone is*

14

focused on the sacrifice of Christ. No one sees that Jesus saved himself before he saved others. He did what was desirable from within Him and forsook all of the expectation that other's thrust upon Him. He believed, He spoke, He lived and then He died. He did not die until after He lived. He did not give up his life, until he had a life worth giving. A life worth living."

Yes. That is the truth. I knew the answer to be the truth that satisfied my soul. I knew there was a message that was beyond the basic concept of sacrifice. There is a time for all things and there is an order. I was not to put death before life. I was not to put the sacrifice before living. It was not my time to die. I still live. That is why if feels so off even though I am told it should feel right. I am not dead, I am yet alive. I cannot and did not come out of the box tied to a cross. I should not wear a cross because it makes me look good or makes everyone else feel good about the cross on their back or the lack thereof. I had a choice standing before me.

It was obvious I had to choose life. What I was living was not life. It was a sacrifice. I could no longer sacrifice myself, my dreams and my life just to cope and make it through because society, religion, culture, and others said so. Who are they? They are not my God.

Making the decision to suck it up meant I would not be myself. The representative in this marriage, in this family, in this life was going to short change everyone. I would be shortchanged in this life. I did not sign up to come to earth to be short changed. I had to be candid with myself.

As much as I loved my life, I hated aspects of it. What is amazing is how those minor facets were often able to cloud the greater good. They were distracters from all that I desired to do and be. I was so heavy and burdened by the everyday routine of my life. The activities that "good" wives and mothers do clouded my day and took away my joy. They stole time I set for myself and separated me from the family I said I was doing everything for. I was lonely, overworked, undervalued and tired. Many times undervalued more by me than anyone else because I did not value the things I was spending energy on. I understood their importance to everyone else or the overall family, but they said nothing about me that was of value to me.

I had someone tell me that *we are doing these trivial undesirable things for everyone and sacrificing for everyone as a gift unto God.* To say I was doing them unto God would be just a line to pacify my sick soul because I was not doing it unto God. *If I was doing something unto God it would not be this*, I kept thinking to myself. If I am to do anything unto God He would be getting some kind of glory out of it as well would He not? I was not getting any joy out of some of the things I was doing, nor did I think they were any gift or glory I was giving God. That was a mind game I chose not to play.

I was too tired to love, too tired to hate, too tired to take time for myself or anyone else. I was mustering the energy to do it one day at a time. Staying strong. Putting on a good face and loathing every minute of it because that is what "strong good" wives, mothers, and women do.

The only time I felt good is when I was present with my family, but not doing anything for them or when I was making speeches and talking to others about what I or they desired. I felt complete when I prayed, read and when I meditated. I could see myself doing all that I desired in my spirit and it pleased me to my core. However, before being frank with myself those meditation sessions did not last long. I was so tired I would fall right to sleep in the middle of the session.

Sleep was my refuge. It was my way to see myself out of today. I could see tomorrow and do anything in my dreams. I was free to be ME. I knew I was in a bad state when sleep was a good thing for me. I don't like to sleep a lot and cannot go to sleep as long as the sun is out, but I was craving naps and the ability to lie down and think of being in another place and doing another thing.

I found myself frustrated with my husband and children because while they sat on the sofa relaxing, I was still doing and going. After working and running around all day I would then go grocery shopping, cooking, giving baths, cleaning and the like. My work seemed to never end. Everyone else was relaxing and I was doing everything to make sure they were relaxing happy. I found myself resenting them sitting there and resenting myself for resenting them and resenting myself for making it easy for them to sit there drinking the drinks I made, eating the food I made and watching the movie I ordered.

I felt lonely in a house full of people. I was lonely in my thoughts, my feelings, my hurt and in the loss of my dream idea of a family, the loss of me. Who could I tell the truth to and how would they take it. I did not want to tell them. I did not want them to take it the wrong way. I just needed someone to hear me. Someone to understand. Someone to be present with me as I walked this through in my head. It felt as if I had no one. After all, I am the "good" and "strong" wife and mother. The ones I needed to tell the most are the ones I felt I could not tell for fear of hurting them. Fear of their reaction. Fear of not being who they wanted me to be.

I wanted to tell them. My issue was that I needed to know for sure that they would say what I most needed to hear. I wanted to hear them say that they could go without me doing and being what they wanted because they desired my presence and my love more than anything else. I wanted a release from being anything other than who I am.

I needed to be sure they got it. It was vital that they saw me as who I am. I am a spirit that desires to experience this gift of life to its greatest extent, just as they desire, in the most limitless capacity. I did not need them to see me as the mom or wife that quit being the limited ideal they had of her. I needed them to know it was not selfish to desire for me to be first in my life, but self-full.

When I am full of me, I can give more of me. I want to live my definition of who I am. I desired to do the things I desire. Somewhere I got lost on the way. That day I found ME. I desired them to validate her as well. To re-member (remember) her with me. To understand that her presence is what I most desired. I knew they would appreciate this more authentic Me than the She that does stuff or conforms to their every want.

Don't get me wrong, I love my family. They are wonderful and I adore them for who they are and cherish the family unit in which we are. My authenticity and my love for them have nothing to do with one another. One does not cancel the other one out. That is what I had to learn. Understanding that will help many of us get to the point of validating self and walking in truth.

When we think it can only be one way or the other in our lives, we miss the complexity of who we are and will fail to encounter the various characteristics of our lives. We are not black or white. We are grey, blue, yellow and everything in between. When we give ourselves permission to be all things and accommodate the expressions of ourselves as we evolve and grow the happier we will be. The less we will put God in a box. When you understand He is all things and can be experienced in many ways and all those ways can elevate you to another level despite what it looks like you will then understand and appreciate yourself in this manner as well.

So to be clear, I like doing things for my family, but I did not and do not want the things that I do to be my job. I am a giver unashamedly. However, I do not like for anyone to expect or assume I am the giver they can take from at any time. To think it is okay and expected of my role to give at any and all times is an expectation that no one should have to live within. It is a place of deficit. No one should be expected to give on demand or out of an empty cup. I do not desire this for another so I should not succumb to the expectation on me and think it well. I do not want it to be expected of me, but appreciated if and when I do it. I desired it to be freely given when I give it freely. I did not desire an on-demand lifestyle. I aspired to kill expectation and invigorate validation, gratitude and appreciation.

It was vital that my family and anyone who loved me knew that I did not want to be trapped in their expectations. It was necessary that they recognized why the wheel was stopping and why I was getting off, because this was not my *will* for ME. I require ME and my time to be Me. There appeared to be no place or time for me or for me with them and I hungered for both more than anything. I compromised too many times to accommodate and it got confused that I am compromise. I yearned to feel valued without having to do anything to have that value except *be* ME. Completely uncompromising Me.

I was rushing to get things done and rushing through my time with my family so I could get to what I needed to do to keep everything on time, in order and within schedule. I was living a nightmare trying to keep and create a dream. I was surrounded by chaos in my mind trying to create peace in my spirit and life.

I knew I had a lot more to me, a light that shined in me. I knew this to be true, but when I felt like my light was not valued, was marginalized in woman, mother or wife traditional roles or anything less than what I knew of myself I felt like I was dying every day.

Though I wanted to be an exceptional woman, mother and wife, I never wanted the traditional role of those things. I never wanted to be a house wife, a typical wife, or trophy wife. I did not want to do the things these wives often did. If that is your choice, God bless you, but just like I choose not to be a brain surgeon or nurse because I don't like blood, guts, poop or any of that other stuff on or around me, I choose not to be a housewife or trophy wife smiling and waiting on anyone or anything hand and foot while smiling and being cute or broke down tired doing it. Cleaning, shopping or cooking on an everyday basis was not my desire. Whew, I am tired just writing that line.

Traditional ideas of these roles were and are contradictory to who I am. There is so much expectation that these ideals are attached to that enjoying others and just being present in many of the moments of life was hardly possible because the person playing any of these roles was usually orchestrating, directing or capturing the moment, and not living it. Since she is the woman, mother, wife, daughter or sister she is expected to sacrifice her joy for the joy of everyone else and create the joy of everyone else's. Everyone else's joy, peace and happiness rest on her shoulders and that is not what I signed up for. I signed up to be present in a more expansive life, not the orchestrator, maintenance woman or dictator of a more expansive life.

I longed to write my own story, my own definition of ME and experience her with everyone else. I longed to set the pace on my path in hopes that those around me would learn from what I do and not what I say do. I did not want my girls to get the wrong idea. I did not want to tell them to be free to be themselves and it will bring them joy, but compromise that truth in my own life and live the lie I was exhibiting as evidence to the contrary.

No matter what we say it is only what we do and how we live that teaches our children. I did not want compromising sacrifice to be taught to them. It may feel good to them at this moment because they are on the receiving end of my giving. However, when they were to switch places it would be a death to them. I did not want the harbored lie to be passed down.

Living the way I had been living was making me and all those around me miserable. Why? Because I was not ME. I was everything and everyone that everybody else desired. I can only be me and manifest my own desire out of who I am within me. I am going to let HER light shine and everyone around me will benefit from the residue of My great light.

The world, my family, anyone or anything else outside of me cannot make me happy and therefore their depiction and definition of who I am as a wife, woman and mother I do not subscribe to. I will make My mark as Me and watch what a glory SHE IS.

When I accepted this truth and was able to share it with my family. The load was lifted and my life opened up and made room for ME again and the space for them overflowed.

What is so crazy is that right after becoming free of the burden of expectation and putting myself in my rightful place in my life I had room to do all the things that were cluttering me out from the beginning. Yes, the cooking, cleaning, running around and the like. Why? Because things were in order. I was in order. I was first.

When your mind and spirit are in order the body and the life it is living will fall into order as well. You will discover what is important and what is not and some things will fall to the side and make even more room for you and the things that are the most important for your life's order and comfort will rise to the top.

In ME He dwells and it is ME who dwells in HIM. If I am not free to be ME I am not free to be one in wholeness with the Father that maketh me great. If I am separate from the greatness I am separate from my peace. Peace was restored and the chaos dissipated in the twinkling of an eye because truth set me free.

I AM Responsible

I AM responsible. That which I am – who and what I am is responsible for who and what I am and will be. I am the creator, guard and gardener of this property I call ME.

The only reason my family was a part of my truth is because they were a part of my first choice. A mirror of my waywardness reflecting back to me the neglect within me. I chose to compromise myself out of my responsibility to me and into their desire of me. I had to call myself out of their dream and into my own. In doing so I had to let them be aware that a choice I had to make for my life was going to impact theirs. That was the only reason they were important to my dialogue, because I had put them in the place of being the god of my universe and now I was taking my rightful place back.

I was making another choice to change the choice I previously made that was not benefiting or assisting in the elevation of that that I am. Who I am is limitless. It is the soul of me that is in the likeness and image of God. It is all knowing, all loving, and all things that God is. It is the truth of who we all are. As God said, *"I Am that I AM."* Meaning He is all things that are, that I am possible of being. There is nothing He is not and nowhere is He not. HE IS and will ALL WAYS Be. This is the image and likeness He made us in, in spirit and in truth. Therefore I am like my father in All Ways.

Out of this place I am responsible for speaking, believing, choosing, creating and manifesting the desire of my soul. So the responsibility to change my life is mine. It is out of my mouth, out of my faith and out of my actions that this change will come. I AM responsible. I make the choices or I do not. Not making the choice is still making a choice.

I am responsible for what is planted in my garden of life. I am the reaper, the sower, the weeder and the treader of my own seed.

I am responsible for the deposits others make on my lawn. I am responsible to clean it up or discard it before it soaks into my soil (soul). I am responsible for what I accept on my lawn even if others are dumping it on their. I am responsible to set up the fence, the no dumping sign, or meeting them in the yard to let them know this is not the yard you will play in. I am the protector of my mind/soul/soil and no one is allowed to treat it like a trash dump. I must tell others to keep their dogs off of my lawn and I establish the policy that no dogs are allowed because I will not be left to clean up the crap of another in my life.

Sometimes our biggest struggle is with our family. Mainly because they really do love us and we love them. However when there are no boundaries we allow them to do in our lives (on our lawn) what we really do not want or appreciate. The only time it will change is when we get tired of being tired of cleaning up and patching bald spots in the lawn of our soul and replanting the seeds of our desires only for it to be trampled again. We must set boundaries on where one can play, where one can walk and where there is no access.

Recognizing that we are responsible and taking the power and control in that awareness is a must. No one outside of us can or will be responsible for our destiny.

I Am Responsible

Workbook

Honesty, Desire and Choice

As we transition through life we are often bombarded with roles and ideals of who we are suppose to be. What we are suppose to aspire to have and what is good and unacceptable. Since I was a child I had my own ideas of who I was and who I was not and how counter they were to society's norms, my church's norms and the norms taught at school or played out by those in position of power or respect. Yet, I often compromised because I was not sure how to be me against the protest of all of the other voices that surrounded me.

My own vision of me became distorted and often transitioned into lock step with the beat of the drums around me. I would say that I would like to be a mother and the assumption was I wanted to be a Leave it to Beaver mom or some other idea they had. I stated I will be rich and the assumption was I desired to an obnoxious snob who thought herself better than others. I confessed I yearned to travel the world and I was told I was restless and needed to learn contentment wherever I was. I eagerly stated I want to be an astronaut and see the universe and I was told by my teacher that only white men do those things. She further urged me to find a more acceptable vision for myself like mother, teacher or nurse.

When we speak our desires or tell people our dream or aspiration they can only create a picture based on their experience, expectations and desires which are usually limiting, full of their fear and disappointment. No one can ever see or comprehend a vision of another that is greater than their own. It is beyond their comprehension. Possibility does not live in the hearts and minds of most. Possibility has died at the foot of those who cannot see past yesterday. Those that walk lockstep with whatever has been and hope not for a better tomorrow because today is acceptable to them.

We must make sure we hold on to our dreams, be honest about them and never let anyone outside of us derail us. Our desires are saying something more about us than what is seen on the surface. If our desire is allowed to be stolen, then our dreams will follow and our souls will grow sick and the dreams and desires it holds wastes away over time out of neglect.

For example, when I say I want to go to Africa different people get different pictures in their heads. Some still see primitive ideals that are based on ill intentioned movies or the news. Others may think of war torn countries of Africa, missionary trips, etc. For those that have visited various countries the idea based on their experience in the countries on the continent of Africa may come to their head which are contrary to those who have never experienced.

Africa is a huge continent with many different countries that speak different languages, have various cultural backgrounds, religions, etc. There is no one place alike. To say the continent's name creates different pictures on the minds of different individuals. None having anything to do with the picture or intent of the one who has spoken their desire of a trip to this location. The one who speaks their desire will often have a totally different vision in mind.

If the one who has the desire allows those outside of her to plan her trip to the destiny she desires it would never match her vision.

The vision created by those outside of her, those she has been in communication with will mimic their idea of what she desires to experience. This would most often end in great disappointment. Why? Because we can only create or recreate an image that is a part of us, a part of our vision, that which is born out of our own mind, experience and ideas. The only way another can birth your desire is to die to themselves and all they know in order to indwell in your nature, take on that nature and birth your desire from this place of oneness.

As females we seem to have mastered this death of self for others and sadly expect full reciprocity. Everyone involved in this arrangement has been sadly dissatisfied.

In order for our vision to be realized we must be honest about who we are and who we are not because the manifestation of our desire will come from within us. No one anywhere outside of us will be able to create the life we love and desire. That vision can only be born out of the place that desires it – from within us, out of our spirit. What we eat will not take away another's hunger and what another drinks will not quench our thirst.

I know that this experience in life is about elevating and experiencing myself in the greatest possibilities of myself. Giving and serving to my detriment and being selfish to the point of not giving or serving anyone but myself for the sheer luxury of non-purposed pleasure and lack of responsibility is the same end of the same stick. One is just the top side and the other the bottom, but still the same end of the stick that profits a man nothing. I did not desire either side of this stick. I desired the balance of self in which I was first in line of my own life.

29

Aware of this truth I asked God to help me be real enough with myself to get out of the life experience I did not desire and back to the one I did desire. I sought to get off of this wheel that kept me bogged down with the trivial traditional contradiction of me. It was key that I get back to the place of being me, a place in which expectation of anything less did not live.

I heard three things from God –

1. Be *honest no matter how much you think it will hurt because truth is the only thing that will set you free.*
2. *Figure out what you most desire and be honest about that desire. Does that desire bring about your greatness and MY Glory or is it selfish indulgence?*
3. *Choose another choice. Choose the truth and the desire that brings about My Glory through you over and over again until it becomes your new nature.*

Step 1 – Honesty

The first step is being honest. No matter how brutal and ugly the truth is, if we are not honest we will never be present in the moment and no one will have the pleasure of knowing and loving us as we are, they will only know the representative of us. We will keep playing a role to get the love that is given to our representative and we will secretly be resentful.

But may I be even bolder in my honesty with you? The resentment often felt will be displaced resentment upon others. The resentment will be transferred to others when in fact we are resentful of ourselves for allowing our own neglect.

Denial of the fact that our happiness rest in our own hand leads many to cheat on those they love, immoderation, alcohol abuse, promiscuity, drug abuse and the like. Many participate in these acts from a very early age not understanding the discontentment and disappointment that is settled within their spirit so they feed it these things to calm the beast inside. All these things are ways of searching for self, balance, peace and all that is absent inside. They distract from answering the questions of contradiction they live in.

Folks often blame alcohol or drugs on their behavior or the hurt or broken trust of an ex-lover, friend of family member, instead of admitting who they are and what they are allowing to happen in their lives are causing them pain and they are dealing with the pain with an outside substance or substitute instead of dealing with the pain or emptiness internally with honesty.

Facing the pain head on is the only way to make it disappear. Folks cheat with someone they are allowed to let their hair down in front of who does not judge them or expect anything of them except who they are in the moment. At least that is the lie they tell themselves, but anyone willing to assist another in lying is lying in other ways as well. They actually don't see this as an opportunity to be with a great person. They have prejudged the other person prior to the rendezvous as an easy damaged object. Usually similar to themselves in brokenness. They are drawn to the weakness because they can play out their weaknesses in, on and with the other party and not feel bad about it. When you are seen as damaged then a little more damage done to you is seen as acceptable by another broken person. Hurt people hurt people so the hurt is expected and produced by all sides.

Not realizing we can make this charade of a dance disappear with one choice we stay on the dance floor dancing to a tune we do not like. By choosing for one moment to be real with whom we say we love – ourselves- we can change it all. The dance would be over.

In order to get real love we must risk all love. The fear of pain in reaction to our truth should never stand in the way of freedom and true love in us or for us. Fear will have us stuck, but the one moment of integrity will have us free.

We often think we have to tear everything and everyone apart in order to be whole. But the real work is within. The easy work is getting everyone outside of us on board. It is we who we have to get on board, stick to the plan and feel complete and whole enough to love ourselves more than others so that we can love them with our *whole* heart and *whole* mind and *whole* soul.

Anyone who does not desire our wholeness just exposed their hand and the real reason they are with us. Staying in relationships and taking on roles we despise for everyone else's pleasure at our cost exposes more about who we are and less about the other person(s) when this is the true lie we choose to live.

We do not have to leave or change the outside to be whole. We only have to own it all in order to be released from the bondage of pain and disappointment caused by our own hand and choice.

Outside acts do not change internal breakdown because who we are and what we are within is still present. Even when everyone else outside of us is gone, we are still here in the midst of it all. *Chaos present in the mind and spirit, though absent from around the body.* This external change is temporary. Whatever is happening in the mind and spirit will eventually mirror itself around and in the body.

When we love we often compromise. That is a given. The problem occurs when we compromise ourselves out of our own dream. I felt compromised out of my own dream at times. I did not want to do the same to others. In order to not cause waves that would cause another to relinquish their desires I deserted mine putting them on the back burner for another day.

Thinking this was a "good" and big thing for me to do was a lie. I was actually saying that I agree with the notion that my desire is not worthy enough to disturb or interrupt another's, but everyone else's is worthy of halting my own. I further victimized myself by abandoning my voice. I was establishing a precedence of how to be treated.

Fear of judgment and the feeling of shame often stop us from saying our desire out loud. Especially if we have so much to be grateful for. However, having a great life does not negate us from changing those aspects that do not bring about our joy and wholeness. We are promised life and life abundantly. I put a demand on that promise. All the good I have will not stop me from desiring to improve, grow and elevate more and more.

Yes I have a lot to be grateful for and I do not regret anything I have or have ever done. I am grateful for it all, even the compromises. Especially the heaviness experienced that birth this truth. It has all awakened me to who I am and who I am not.

The pressure I was putting on myself and allowing to be placed on me by others was distorting my truth of who I desired to be for ME. It clouded all of the wonderful things I was and had. It was a fracture in my wholeness.

Getting over the fear of how our truth sounds and how others will take it is hard to get over. However, truth is truth and when it is truth and not blame or judgment then it will set us free every time and heal us where we are broken.

This book is not about judgment or blaming my family, society or anything or anyone else outside of me, because the truth is my choice and my choices alone had me standing in the place I did not desire. This is about realizing why you are where you are and how to make another choice. You cannot go where you desire to go unless you understand why you are not there already. I had to have the tools to create the life that blessed Me. One of those tools is knowledge. Knowledge to know what to do and what not to do again.

When I finally told my husband what I was feeling and the change I needed to make he just listened. I was not looking for quick fixes or direction or information. I needed him to hear me. I needed to get everything circling within me out. His ear and presence was important to me because I needed him to see ME again and hear the pain of me losing my way.

He did and he was everything I needed him to be in that moment. He was actually relieved because he could see there was something changing within me that was contrary to my personality. He was pleased and comforted by my words, my revelation, my truth and the light of ME returning as the weight was lifted during my reaffirmation.

We established a new choice together out of the choices I had made for myself as he was given insight into my mind and soul. The support, appreciation and consideration were everything I desired. He was so on point that because I loved him for being everything I needed in that moment I almost did what I usually do in response to his graciousness and loving persona. As he capitulated to my desire, I walked backwards and said – *"Oh, no you don't have to change anything or do anything for me. I just wanted to tell you how I felt. Don't worry about it, don't worry about me. I will figure it all out."*

I could have slapped myself in the mouth for just thinking the thought. I heard the voice of God speak as I caught this utterance escaping my mouth – God said "you *got what you asked for and you are willing to throw it back? Pay attention to the habit you have created. It has become your first nature, make another choice. Keep making that choice until this new nature is your first nature. The nature in which who I AM is first.*"

I had to walk back on my statement and affirm right there my own desire for me and accept the hand of the one I loved. The hand I longed for. The one who is the other half of the foundation for my family. The heart that was in lockstep with my drum in that moment more so than any time before. I accepted his support and recognition of my new choice.

Right there my truth had set me free and I almost fell back into the hole. But thank God, no really, THANK GOD. I saw my own hand being my own enemy compromising me out of my promise. I owned the mistake and in turn I was able to disown all that that mistake was stealing from me.

We will never be free or live our truth if we are always conforming. What we continue to bend to will be our god and we will do whatever it takes to keep the company of our god. The fear of losing any of our graven images will keep our truth shut up in us and we will compromise and become dis-eased from the inside out until we let truth out of our mouth. We have to risk giving up our gods in order for the God in us to be free to shine out of us and our greatness to be displayed. The question becomes what do we love more, ourselves or our graven image? Which love will make us free?

****

What areas of your life have you compromised? Why?

_____
_____
_____
_____
_____

What do you really feel? If you knew no one would be hurt by what you desire to confess what would you say? Why?

_____
_____
_____
_____
_____

Who do you feel will be hurt by your truth? Why?

_____
_____
_____
_____
_____

What do you fear will be the consequence of your truth?

_____
_____
_____
_____
_____

What do you fear will be the consequence if you are not honest about your truth?

_____

_____

_____

_____

_____

What fear do you have about stopping this compromise forever? What could you lose? What could you gain?

_____

_____

_____

_____

_____

Which consequence do you think you could live with of the two – the lose or the gain?

_____

_____

_____

_____

_____

Which consequence will bring you the freedom to be who you are?

_____

_____

_____

_____

_____

Do you choose yourself?

_____
_____
_____
_____
_____

Who is the god of your universe? What rules you?

_____
_____
_____
_____
_____

2- My Highest Desire

A want is a longing, a hunger, craving or ache for something you do not have. That means it is outside of you and you do not possess it. Your desires are within you. It is what is in your heart or soul that desires to manifest. When God, the supply, breathed himself in you He breathed the supply of all things within you. Therefore you are lacking nothing. You are whole and complete. All that you desire you can have because it is already yours. You are always birthing what is in your spirit and heart and manifesting it into your life. When you are in want you believe it is out of your power to manifest.

When you realize that the power to choose and create a different life or outcome is within you then you can and will make another choice. You will operate in the laws and principles of manifestation to bring about new life and life abundantly. When you can't see or see distorted you think that the power is outside of you. You feel powerless to make a change and continue to be in want as you name yourself to be. You name yourself-I am want- and therefore you take on the nature of wanting. When you name yourself newness, choice, difference, unique, peace, joy, love, prosperity, success, etc you take on the nature of your new name by choosing to be that new desire of who you are.

When you have a desire, choose it. Get your mind and body to line up with the soul's desire. Your soul inhabits the mind of God and the truth of who you are. Often your mind and body are rejecting this truth because it fears from past experience based on earthly knowledge.

Your soul may say this is who you are, tell the truth and be free. But your mind may think this person can't handle it, I don't want to deal with the outcome and your body is thinking oh no, the thought of it is making me tight and I can't pass the air in the lungs so since we are stressed already, if you don't want to do it mind, then I, the body does not either because I am already not feeling well.

You have to tell your mind, we are going to deal with the truth and submit to the soul so I can be free and then tell the body, it will be swift even if painful, but we have been through a lot of things and we are still here so we can handle it. Once you get them behind the soul instead of the soul behind the mind and body you will be in sync and the courage to be who you are will show up in the moment because you know you are operating in truth and your highest desire for yourself.

******

What is your greatest desire? What nature do you desire to be and give?

_____

_____

_____

_____

_____

What does it look like? Who benefits from the nature of your desire? How?

_____

_____

_____

_____

_____

How will you manifest this desire when given the opportunity?

_____

_____

_____

_____

_____

How do your soul, mind and body feel about this desire?

_____

_____

_____

_____

_____

3 – Choose Another Choice

I made the choice to conform and put my desires on the back burner, hoping one day my time would come in the midst of doing and giving to everyone else.

That is all it was going to be was a hope. In order for us to get change we have to operate in the Law of Choice. I had to choose another choice for myself. Not hope it, not wish it, not thing about it, not pray on it, but choose it.

Before making that choice I had to define what it is I desired. I had to write a vision for myself and see it by meditating on it day and night. When you mediate on a vision you can see it for what it is. Life will not just happen with your best interest in mind. You do not want to live as a reaction to life. You can become the creator of it by *seeing* it first.

You can *see* the pitfalls and the greatness of your vision by walking in it. When you meditate on it and see that it is good, then choose that good choice. Name it to be who you are. Tell yourself that you are not a reactor, you are a creator and this is the life you desire and choose it to be so. It is who you are. You are that choice. Every time something comes to counter that thought continue to make the same choice and say, no, I am that choice. That is who I am, not this or the other, I am that. And when you meditate on that new choice feel the new feeling of freedom, peace, joy, prosperity and love. See the feeling and the choice as one and live in that place as if it is already done.

******

What is your desire for yourself?

_____
_____
_____
_____
_____

What is your vision?

_____
_____
_____
_____
_____

What are the details that make this vision great?

_____
_____
_____
_____
_____

What are your boundaries?

_____
_____
_____
_____
_____

What are your goals?

_____
_____
_____
_____
_____

If this choice was present now what would it feel like? What feeling do you feel when you mediate on this choice day and night?

_____
_____
_____
_____
_____

Capture that feeling, look down at your hands and feet and see yourself standing in that choice and feeling. See it as already done. Hear the words you would hear in that moment and react to those words. What does it look and feel like when you are standing in the place of completion of the choice you made?

_____
_____
_____
_____
_____

What else will this choice impact? How will you choose the outcome of the impact in other areas of your life?

_____
_____

_____

_____

_____

4 - What You Resist Persist

Resistance stems from two places. The first is from within us. These are internal struggles. The ideas we hold as the foundation of our belief systems can often be the same thing holding us back from our next level. We are loyal to our families so we want to be loyal to their ways of thinking and operating. We think that if we let go of their way of being, then we dishonor them or even ourselves. Who are we without these beliefs given to us by those we love and trust? You are that you are.

The answer to this question is often frightening and keeps folks holding onto what does not benefit them. Especially if our experiences appear to support these ideas. To overcome these preconceived ideas we have to ask ourselves hard questions. Do we believe what we have been told or thought because of what our eyes or the words of others have told us or do we believe the ears of our soul and eyes of our spirit?

The second place the resistance rises from is from outside of us. I usually say that the struggle is within or without. If it is from the outside or without you then it is a judgment, a norm or idea that others outside of you have agreed upon for whatever reason. You have to ask yourself whether their ideas, norms or roles are good or bad for you and who you desire to be.

These norms or defining roles our societies subscribe to are not usually created and defined with you in mind. They were established without you and the possibility of you in mind, but a greater purpose that served those that pushed forth its existence.

This brings about another question. Do you now subscribe to an idea or definition that did not have your ability, purpose, gift or idea of self in mind? Do you now kill the truth of who you are in order to subscribe to another's that was so limiting it had no idea of the possibility of you and named your possibility impossible and wrong for even believing possible?

The more I knew of me from within and the God within me and the infiniteness of Him in, through and around me and all of life the greater the excitement of myself evolved.

I must stop resisting what limits me. I can no longer allow it to persist in its hold on me. I had to make another choice. Create a plan and vision for myself that manifest who I am.

I recognized my resistance and I blessed the struggle for its awareness and truth exposure. I turned to the God in me and made another choice. I went into the secret place of my soul and planted the vision of my desire and moved on choosing it, blessing it and letting it go to manifest in my life.

I choose me and my idea of me and I accept her for who she is because she is good enough, worthy enough and blessed enough to have all that she desires and she desires only for what is for HER. I only desire me and all that is for me and the manifestation through me that shows the glory and capacity of the limitless God in me. I no longer struggle with the greatness He says that I am. I own it, I choose it so that I may experience the greatness that I am.

****

What are you resisting?

_____
_____
_____
_____
_____

Why Do You Resist It?

_____
_____
_____
_____
_____

Is the struggle within or from outside of you (without you)?

_____
_____
_____
_____
_____

What do you know to be true of you?

_____
_____
_____
_____
_____

What is your choice today?

_____
_____
_____
_____
_____

Who is SHE? What is her purpose? What is her desire to manifest?

_____
_____
_____
_____
_____
_____
_____
_____

What is your plan to make it so?

_____
_____
_____
_____
_____
_____
_____
_____
_____
_____
_____
_____

_____

_____

_____

_____

This is MY truth today:

_____

_____

_____

_____

_____

_____

_____

_____

_____

_____

_____

_____

_____

_____

_____

_____

_____

_____

_____

_____

_____

_____

_____

_____

_____

_____

_____

_____

_____

_____

_____

Notes:

_____

_____

_____

_____

_____

_____

_____

_____

_____

_____

_____

_____

_____

_____

_____

_____

_____

_____

_____

_____

_____

_____

_____

_____

_____

_____

_____

_____

_____

_____

_____

_____